Barcelona

EVEREST

Text: Luis Miracle Arola

Photographs: Miguel Raurich, Juan José Pascual
and Archivo Everest

Editorial coordination: Francisco Bargiela

Diagrams: José Manuel Núñez

Cover Design: Alfredo Anievas

Digital image processing: Marcos R. Méndez

Cartography: © Everest

Translation: Alfredo Álvarez

© EDITORIAL EVEREST, S.A.
Carretera León-La Coruña, km 5 - LEÓN
ISBN: 84-241-2986-5
Legal deposit: LE. 239-1999
Printed in Spain

EDITORIAL EVERGRÁFICAS, S.L.
Carretera León-La Coruña, km 5
LEÓN (Spain)

The Palau Sant Jordi, the work of the Japanese architect Arata Isozaki, is an example of the most advanced engineering.

Barcelona, extolled as the *grand enchanter* by the poet Joan Maragall, exerts this charm not only in everyday life but also when it takes centre stage and hosts one the world's great events: the **Universal Exhibition,** the **International Exhibition,** the **Olympics** (rated in their time as *the best ever held*), etc.

The city prides itself on its vitality and innovating drive and these very qualities have won it great praise, as when Eduardo Mendoza chose it as the setting for one of his novels and dubbed it therein the *City of the Prodigies.*

But it has not entirely escaped criticism. Maragall himself, in the same *Oda nova a Barcelona,* calls it *vana i coquina* (frivolous and mean). Nonetheless, the visitors who flock to see it today will not have such negative thoughts in mind but will rather be keen to capture, albeit fleetingly, some of the features that make up its personality, to see the sights handed down by its long history, to appreciate the efforts made to shape its future, to enjoy any of the attractions it offers: in short, to make the most of their stay, however brief may be the time they can spend there. The following texts are designed to be a compendium of these essential features, leaving it up to the reader to choose those most suited to the time he has available.

TRACES OF A ROMAN PAST

Proud as it may be of some aspects of its
present-day reality, Barcelona preens itself no
less on its historical roots. Indeed it can claim
to be two thousand years old, since, apart from
proven links with Carthaginian settlers, its
origins have also been traced back to a
settlement established by Roman colonisers of
Layetania in the first century B.C. Under the
command of Augustus these founded the
colony of *Julia Augusta Paterna Faventia
Barcino* around the mound known as *Mons
Taber* on the slopes of today's Montjuic.
Exhibits of this imperial origin and the
subsequent development of the colony can be
seen in the **Museu d'Historia de la Ciutat,** City
History Museum, housed in one of the Gothic
buildings bordering the Plaça del Rei. Strictly
speaking, this is the old house *Clariana
Padellás,* brought here brick by brick when the
opening up of the Via Laietana revealed the
remains of a C4th century street of the *Barcino.*
The preservation of this archaeological treasure
in the basement of the museum therefore
affords us the chance today of strolling through
a section of that remote past.
But vestiges of this part of its history can also
be seen in broad daylight. The **walls** raised in
the C3rd to protect the original city still stand
today, albeit partially, in some streets and
squares of the inner city. The best example is
the redoubtable section that stands in the lower
part of the building at the rear of the capilla de
Santa Ágata in the Plaça de Ramon Berenguer
el Gran, and in the extension formed by Carrer
de Tapinería. This Roman legacy is rounded off
by the remains of a necropolis, its underground
tombs lined up beneath the Plaça de la Vila de
Madrid, at the end of Carrer de Canuda in the
upper part of La Rambla. Four striking columns
with Corinthian capitals, presumed to date
from the C1st and attributed to an Augustinan
Temple, can also be seen in the patio of the
Gothic building housing the **Centre
Excursionista de Catalunya** in Carrer de
Paradís.

View of Barcelona with the Port.

Capilla Real de Santa Àgata.

PEACEFUL ROMANESQUE CORNERS

A modest-looking hermitage standing on the corner of a small square at the start of Carrer de Montcada, before this crosses Carrer de la Princesa, will take the visitor back to the sober lines characterising the Catalan Romanesque style of the C12th. This chapel was built in 1166 on the initiative of a trader called *Marcús,* by whose name it is generally known despite having been officially dedicated to the **Virgen de la Guía.**

This dedication to "la Guía", or guidance stems from the fact that this spot, then outside the walls, used to be the last stop of the post coach before it left the city. Today the chapel has been restored and cleansed of the cloying details subsequently added. It may be visited, but only for devotional purposes, at certain hours of the morning.

Not far off, in the same district of Ciutat Vella, following Carrer de Carders and its continuation in Carrer de Basses de Sant Pere, stands another building of Romanesque origin, the convent of **Sant Pere de les Puelles,** also called the convent of the *Doncellas* (maidens) to mark the fact that it is a nunnery. Its origins date right back to an early C9th chapel, but later extraneous additions make it hard to classify as authentically Romanesque; details of this style, however, are evident in such features as the cloister columns and capitals.

The **Church of Sant Pau del Camp** has enjoyed a kinder fate, conserved in the site of what was its monastery hard by the Ronda de Sant Pau and the Avinguda del Parallel. Today the church is set in gardens, fruit of a later reform. The monastery was standing in the C10th and did not escape the ravages of the Arab leader Almanzor when he sacked the city in 985. The church itself was reconstructed in 1117 and thereafter repeatedly restored down the ages until ending up with its aspect of today. Fortunately the harmonious architecture of the cloister has remained untouched, with its lobed arches and twin columns, which engender between them an atmosphere of utter peace.

A SYMBOLIC CITY CENTRE

One of the main attractions of a visit to
Barcelona is without doubt to be found in the
Barri Gotic (Gothic District), which contains a
number of buildings belonging to this period,
but also to the Baroque and Renaissance.
Starting with the former, the visitor can begin
his tour in the **Plaça de Sant Jaume,** where he
will find an initial example in the facade of the
Palau de la Generalitat (seat of regional
Catalan government) in Carrer de Sant
Honorat. Its stern lines contrast with the
ornamental richness across the way in Carrer
de Bisbe, where the most important feature is a
splendid medallion depicting the **imagen del
caballero San Jorge** (the knight Saint George),
one of the recurring themes of Catalan
sculpture.

Plaça del Rei.

*Sculpture of Sant Jordi
in the "Pati dels Tarongers" of the Generalitat.*

At first sight this Flamboyant Gothic style seems to
be continued in the ornate bridge linking the
palau with one of the Baroque houses of the
Canonges (Canons) on the other side of Carrer del
Bisbe, which is the official residence of the
President of the Catalan Government.
Appearances in this case are deceptive, however,
and this construction is in fact a Neogothic
creation of 1928. If you have a chance to visit the
palau, availing yourself of one of the very few
days when it opens its doors to the public, you
will be able to see a number of original Gothic
features, including the staircase, the rosy columns
and the arches of the inner courtyard, the
gargoyles and corbels with their singular outlines,
the dazzling Flamboyant Gothic doorway of the
Capilla de Sant Jordi, or the *Cambra Daurada,*
and the graceful *Pati dels Tarongers* (Courtyard of
the Oranges), in which Gothic elements are
combined with Renaissance features.

In remaining rooms, pride of place goes to the elegant twentieth century design of the **Salón Torres García,** in marked contrast with the grandiose chromatic formalism of the Salón de Sant Jordi. The **Ajuntament** (City Hall) faces the palau across the square. It also has a Gothic style facade, the one on Carrer de la Ciutat. This facade also boasts a handsome sculpture representing the Archangel San Rafael, the work of Pere Ça Anglada. Access into this building, which houses pieces of great artistic value, especially sculptures and pictorial decorations, is also limited to special occasions, usually coinciding with one of the city festivals.

This square is only a stone's throw from the one that can be said to be symbolic of this medieval district: the **Plaça del Rei,** reached by Carrer Llibreteria and Carrer Veguer. Looming large in the foreground is the great staircase leading from the flagstone pavement up to the entrance of the Palau Reial Major. The latter boasts the handsome **Capilla de Santa Àgata,** with the statue of the young martyr and the famous altarpiece of the Condestable (Constable), the work of Jaume Huguet. The solemn **Salón del Tinell** alongside disputes with the Badalona Monastery of Sant Jeroni de la Murtra the honour of being the place where, beneath the sweeping arches, the Catholic Monarchs, Ferdinand and Isabella, received Christopher Columbus on his return from "that voyage that doubled the earth", as Verdauger says in his verses dedicated to Barcelona.

Above: Salón del Tinell.

Right: Ajuntament (City Hall).
Salón de Cent (Council Chamber).

Casa de l'Ardiaca in Barri Gotic.

The district also has other Gothic buildings that are well worth a visit: the **Church of Sant Just y Sant Pastor,** in the Plaça de Sant Just close to the Plaça de Sant Jaume, deemed to be the oldest church in Barcelona (1346); the **Casa de L'Ardiaca** (Archdeacon) on the corner of the Plaça de la Seu, with its fine, cloister-like courtyard and the eye-catching mailbox added by its restorer Domènech i Montaner: the **Pia Almoina** on the opposite side of the same square, site of the Museo Diocesano, an essential visit if only to see its valuable collection of pieces belonging to the artistic heritage of the church.

The lovely **Church of Sant Sever,** which stands behind the Palau de la Generalitat, is Baroque in style, as is the Church of **Sant Felip Neri** in the square of the same name, an enchanting spot among the alleyways surrounding the cathedral.

Nearby stands a five-storey tower of a regular floor plan with a series of small arches on each floor, which is informally known as Atalaya del Rey Martí. (Lookout of King Martí). Also close by is the **Museo Marès,** although the entrance is to be found on the small square of Sant Lu, next to the cathedral. This museum, whose wealth of contents will no doubt be an agreeable surprise, has an inner courtyard where orange trees and a quaint pond offer a haven of peace that will delight those who wish to take a break here in their tour. The Palau del Lloctinent (Deputy) is a restrained but nonetheless majestic building joined onto the museum.

Finally, the aforementioned **Museu d'Historia de la Ciutat** completes the set of Gothic buildings surrounding the square. The upper floors of this building give access in summer to the surrounding flat rooftops, offering a night-time stroll through their narrow passageways and thereby affording unique views of the illuminated city. The voluminous non-figurative sculpture set on one corner of the square, called Topos, (moles) is the work of the contemporary artist Eduardo Chillida.

Antique shop in Barri Gotic.

Cathedral of Santa Creu. ▶

Interior of the Cathedral.

OF DEVOTION AND ART

The visitor observing the buildings of the Barri Gotic will no doubt have noticed one of the main features of Barcelona architecture of this style: the emphasis placed on horizontal lines in contrast with the verticality of the contemporary buildings of northern Europe. There are few exceptions to this trend, but one building that does break the general rule, with its spiky towers and pointed pinnacles, is the **Catedral de la Santa Creu i de Santa Eulàlia.** But the predominant vertical line of its façade is due to a specific reason: these, so to speak, heterodox parts were added on in the second half of the C19th, and although they did indeed follow a medieval design they were built under the orders of a Norman master builder.

The **Capilla de Santa Llúcia** (1257-1258) also belongs to this epoch; it is an intimate chapel for private prayer, giving onto the cloister. Its devotional function is immediately obvious upon crossing its threshold and entering the impressive, soaring nave and aisles of an obviously pure Gothic style. Paying due respect to those who pause to say a prayer before the main altar and chapels, where they leave lighted candles as charming offerings, the visitor is spoilt for choice in terms of artistic treasures to see. Fortunately he is aided by some explanatory plaques before each of the chapels offering a detailed description of the contents in several languages, whether these be statues and tombs, distinguished pieces carved in marble or alabaster or altarpieces of the extraordinary Gothic Catalan painting school, pride of place going to that of San Cosme and San Damián and the one known as the Transfiguration, both by Bernat Martorell.

It is well worth hiring the services of an expert guide, who will offer both individuals and groups, in their chosen language, the chance of appreciating in detail all the following features: the magnificent Choir, with its choir-stalls related to the order of the Toisón de Oro and sculptural work in wood of Pere Ça Anglada, also present in the pulpit; the exquisite retrochoir, in part the work of Bartolomé Ordóñez; the intimate, Italianate lines of the crypt of Santa Eulàlia; the solemnity of the chapel of Cristo de Lepanto; the details of the cloister, with a courtyard adorned by ancient trees and plants and with a central fountain where, during the festival of *Corpus Christi,* and to the delight of all the local children, the spectacle called ou com balla is held, involving an egg shell dancing on a jet of water.

The **Sala Capitular** (Chapter House), set among the chapels of this cloister, houses a small but priceless cathedral museum. Its exhibits, both paintings and sculptures, include such treasures as the altarpiece of the Pietà, the work of Bartolomé Bermejo, and also the works in precious metal kept in the Treasury in a room next to the sacristy. The Cathedral building, like that of Pia Almoina, has a lift to take visitors to the upper floors where they can enjoy an impressive view of the surroundings.

Cathedral Cloister.

Not even the figures adorning the doorway arches can claim to be Gothic. They were made by Agapit Vallmitjana, a brilliant disciple of the Neo-classical sculptor Damià Campeny who, together with his brother Venanci, was producing the best Catalan sculpture in the late C19th. Authentic medieval work, therefore, will have to be looked for in other doorways, like that of the **Puerta de Sant Lu,** the oldest, or that of **Santa Eulália** and **Pietat,** which lead into the cloister, the three dating from the C13th and built in the transitional Romanesque-Gothic style.

THE QUEEN'S RETREAT

The young Catalan noble Elisenda de Montcada, queen by virtue of her marriage to Jaime II el Justo, had no choice but to accept the fact that the latter preferred to fix the place for his eternal rest in the Monastery of Santes Creus in a tomb next to another containing the remains of his first wife Blanca de Anjou. Perhaps in compensation for this frustration, Elisenda was thereafter granted the royal concession of land and property, on a high spot on the fringes of the city, to build a convent to house her own tomb and to serve her as a retreat in case she should become a widow, which eventuality indeed came to pass in 1327. The work began a year earlier and was carried through quickly, so the building has an overall unified style. The church was consecrated shortly after the king's death and after a while the *Reina de Pedralbes* was able to enter the Convent of Pedralbes to live out her days with the Franciscan nuns of Sant Clara, to whom she herself had granted custody. Albeit only partially, this community of the Order of Saint Clare still occupies the site today. Throughout the centuries both convent and church have suffered many ups and downs in their fortunes, including total abandonment during the Spanish civil war. Both came unscathed out of the war by virtue of the timely intervention of the Barcelona authorities, and today the whole group constitutes one of the most illustrious examples of Catalan Gothic architecture.

The **Cruz (cross) de Pedralbes,** set in the upper part of the avenue of the same name that runs into the Diagonal, serves as a precursor of the convent itself. It is mainly famed for having one of the most spacious cloisters of its style. And indeed the superb three-tiered rectangle is a paradigm of the balance and harmony of medieval architecture, well worth the visit in itself. Its two lower tiers have a delicate series of pointed arches supported on stylised twin columns. Its other attractions include the chance of viewing the daytime cells occupied in the olden days by the nuns. These touching examples of patent sobriety are laid out along the length of the cloister. One of them, belonging to the abbess Francesca Saportella, has a chapel of Sant Miguel whose walls are adorned with paintings by Ferrer Bassa, captivating both for their drawing and colour and clearly influenced by the Italian Gothic school of Giotto di Bondone.

Convent of Pedralbes.

A tour through the remaining rooms opened to the public by the nuns of St Claire gives the visitor an insight into the smallest details of the retired life. Besides aspects related to convent life itself, the visitor will also note other details such as the scenes of the life of Jesus by Catalan nativity scene creators, to be found in a room next to the procurator's office. But what can safely be said to be the climax of the visit is the art collection of Thyssen-Bornemisza, now housed in an old dormitory specially fitted-out for the purpose. Works from the German and Italian Renaissance, from the Venetian Baroque and paintings by Fra Angelico, Cranach, Titian, Tintoretto, Rubens, Canaletto, etc., more than vouch for the museum's quality. The main features of the church itself, open only on days of worship and during the services, are the delicate stained-glass windows and, in the presbytery, the alabaster tomb of the founder.

Salón Neoclásico of the Picasso Museum.

OF NOBLES AND ARTISANS

A short way from the Via Laietana, opening onto Carrer de la Princesa, is an area of evident historical pedigree: the **Carrer de Montcada,** which flourished during many years of the medieval and modern era as families of the Catalan nobility decided to build in this street their residential mansions from the C13th to C17th. These diverse Gothic, Renaissance and Baroque mansions, in their day components of an aristocratic and stately area, still stand out today in a more or less perfect state of preservation as you stroll through the narrow pedestrian precinct. Art has always been nurtured in this area of galleries and museums, and this has helped it to maintain its distinguished air intact right up to our days.

The star turn is undoubtedly the **Picasso Museum,** one of the most visited museums in Barcelona and its prime tourist and cultural attraction. It stands head and shoulders above its competitors because, apart from a wealth of works by Picasso himself, it also includes a varied selection of works by artists representative of the different epochs and styles in which Picasso worked, an artist now universally recognised as part of world heritage. The mansions of Bereguer de Aguilar, and of Barón de Castellet y Meca, which house this exceptional collection, stand out in their own right as prime examples of the non-religious architecture of the C13th and C14th.

Different stages in Picasso's pictorial work:
The First Communion, Bust Figure of Woman with Hat and The Divan.

Courtyard of Palau Dalmases in Carrer de Montcada.

The mansion of the Marqueses de Llió y Nadal, which houses the **Textile and Costumes Museum** and the **Precolumbian Museum,** belongs to the same period, though in this case with obvious Renaissance and Baroque additions.

Both here and in the Picasso Museum there is a particularly appealing café cum restaurant opening off the arches that make up the interior courtyard.

The **Palau Dalmases,** headquarters of a Catalan cultural entity, allows the visitor to see just inside the lobby an exquisitely sculpted staircase, which is one of the gems of Catalan Baroque ornamentation.

Galleries containing contemporary art and shops with one overall atmosphere and a variety of products round off the character of the street, where architectural works of international merit rub shoulders with simple but delightful examples of popular craftsmanship.

It is the Barcelona of the crafts guilds and craftsmanship that seems to regale you as you walk through this area, which then leads on to one of the prime Gothic monuments in the city: the **Church of Santa María del Mar.**
Here it was the shipowners, the *bastaixios de ribera* or porters who took it upon themselves to build the church between 1329 and 1390, with the final and conclusive intervention of Pedro III el Ceremonioso.
Although access can be gained from the back part of the church, to which we have arrived, it is the main door, to the west, that affords the best vision of its striking interior: the lofty nave and aisles forming a single body, separated off

Interior of the Church of Santa Maria del Mar.

Bell tower of the Church of Santa Maria del Mar, seen from Pla del Palau.

by sturdy octagonal columns that reinforce the overall impression of solidity and majesty. A great rose window at the back and many stained-glass windows at the sides add a dash of colour to the severe lines of this church, recognised as one of the great achievements of Mediterranean Gothic.
The best time to visit the church is during the celebration of a religious service, when the lighting comes into its own, or during a musical recital, to hear its excellent acoustics. The tour can be finished off in the streets surrounding the adjacent
Passeig del Born, abounding in art galleries and studios.

On this page and the two preceding ones: different views of the Plaça de Catalunya.

MARKETS AND ANTIQUE SHOPS AROUND SANTA MARÍA DEL PI

It is in the lower part of the **Plaça de Catalunya,** the starting point of this tour, that the street spectacles befitting all great cities are concentrated, especially at the weekends, helping to liven up the inner city and especially the old part.

Polished musical *troupes* or simply eager amateurs, many foreign from exotic spots, earn their daily bread by setting up their pitch in any part of the square, from where their performances overflow into the adjacent Avinguda del Portal de l'Angel. The visitor will note that this last stretch has been renovated with rather unfortunate results, especially in the use of uncomfortable concrete blocks for sitting on.

From the Gothic fountain, which shows some attractive twentieth century murals of the ceramist Aragay, the visitor can choose from many alternative routes. The first is to take Carrer dels Arcs to the Plaça Nova where we can appreciate the sgraffito sketch with which Picasso decorated the facade of the Catalunya Architects College, a sparing but highly evocative version of a Catalan popular tradition.

A lovely contre jour effect in Plaça de Catalunya.

Another option is to take the Carrer de Cucurulla and then turn down Carrer de Portaferrissa to enter the narrow Carrer de Petritxol, once a bustling area where everyone thronged to try out its dairies and drinking chocolate cafés. The charm of small shops still reigns here, interspersed with select art galleries. Ceramic wall plaques with witty drawings and rhymes pay homage to famous citizens who lived or were born in the building in question, and also touch upon themes reflecting a flourishing past.

By whichever option our route ends up in the set of three squares surrounding the **Church of Santa María del Pi,** a sturdy Gothic construction with marked horizontal lines. Built between the C14th and C15th, it is considered to be one of the three best Gothic buildings in Barcelona. The great rose window that seems to swamp the upper part of the facade has a magnificent display of stained glass, reproductions of the originals destroyed in 1936. The interior, equally affected by the disturbances of that time and subsequently restored, contains the altar and tomb of the miracle worker and preacher Sant Josep Oriol, who performed laying on of hands in the Capilla de la Sang in the late C17th. The three aforementioned squares, Plaza del Pi, Plaza Sant Josep Oriol and the "placita" or small square of Pi, are venues for soaking up the sun in café chairs set out for that purpose, for visiting the small street markets selling natural products, second-hand objects and antiques or the open-air art shows by painters who set up their pitches on Thursdays, Saturdays and Sundays. The artistic attractions are rounded off by the long-standing antique shops in the surrounding streets of Banys Nous and de la Palla.

The Plaça Reial, with the Three Graces Fountain.

The Plaça Reial, a favourite spot for soaking
up the sun at one of the café tables under the arches,
is also one of the prime sites for street artists.

Bird's eye view of La Rambla, with the Columbus Monument in the foreground.

A MEDITERRANEAN ATMOSPHERE

La Rambla is by far and away the most typical and popular site in Barcelona for taking a stroll. It is almost a cliché by now to stress its cosmopolitan character, but the truth is that the colourful atmosphere to be found beneath its lofty, leafy plane trees is the very essence of Mediterranean cities. The activities of successive stretches even seem to be *preprogrammed,* each with a different name, from the start in Plaça de Catalunya to Portal de la Pau in the port. In the upper part, presided over by the popular talisman of the fountain of Canaletes, some seats – *to be paid for –* mark out the spot where people come together to hold ad lib debates about politics or sport.

Then come the market stalls, first selling pets then the florists that have made La Rambla famous and continue to add their dash of vivid colour.

Next come the living statues, or as they would say *athletes of stillness* who offer representations of the most imaginative characters. There are also puppeteers and street musicians, with a predominance of South American folk music.

Next in line are the portrait artists, complete with easels and sometimes with fictitious models as bait to lure in the passers by.

La Rambla.

Lastly, in the stretch formed by the Rambla de Santa Mónica, a street market of handicrafts and popular products finishes off this always busy, bustling and lively world with some surprising touches. The visitor will have the chance during his stroll to take in architectural and artistic points of great merit. The western side offers the following buildings: the **Church of la Virgen de Betlem,** a restored Baroque building on the corner of Carrer del Carmen; the **Palau de la Virreina** on the Rambla de las Flores, with Rococo architecture and decorative elements, all of which we may see as it serves as a cultural centre of the City Council and may therefore be entered; the facade of the **Gran Teatro del Liceo,** the only part spared by the recent fire, is today being restored and extended; the **Mercado modernista de la Boqueira,** is worth a visit in itself to see the attractiveness of the market stalls and the deftness with which they are attended; the meeting point designed in ceramic by Miró is to be found in the adjacent Pla de la Boquería.

Mime artist and a living statue in La Rambla.

Next comes the **Centro de Arte Santa Mónica,** a gallery showing the most advanced examples of contemporary art; and finally the extraordinary **Reials Drassanes** (Royal Arsenals), one of the most noteworthy of all Barcelona Gothic constructions, not only because of the dockyard equipment, belonging to a medieval shipyard already operating in 1243 and placed at the service of the city in 1935, but also because it is the site of a very important **Maritime Museum.**

As for the eastern side, la Rambla offers, on the corner of Carrer de Portaferrissa, the **Palau Moja,** Neoclassical in design and today occupied by the heritage services of the Generalitat; the **Casa Bruno Quadras,** of exotic modernist decoration standing on Pla de la Boquería; the **Palau neoclásico de Marc,** on the Rambla de Santa Mónica, is also given over to offices of the Generalitat; next to it stands the fascinating **Wax Museum.**

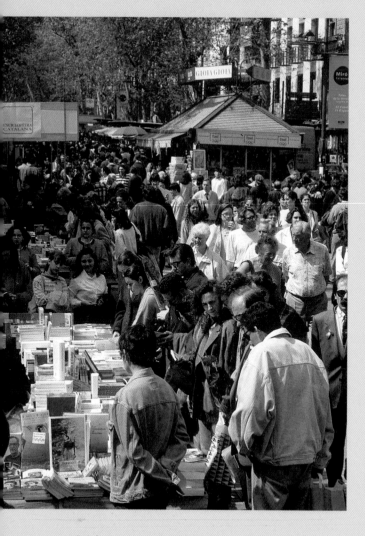

Book Day in La Rambla.

Palau Moja.

Wax Museum.

Flower stalls on La Rambla de las Flores.

Below: Mercado de la Boqueria.

On the following page: Casa Amattler and Casa Batlló.

THE BOURGEOIS BOULEVARD

Until well into the twentieth century, **Passeig de Gràcia** was the residential heart of the Barcelona bourgeoisie, as the boulevard dividing the *Ensanche* or urban expansion area into two halves.

Occupied in the postwar periods almost entirely by banks, it has gradually modified its aspect with more and more shops opening up and bars and restaurants that spread their awnings over the pavement.

These shops include firms of international renown, both in the world of fashion and in that of jewellery and clock-making.

Also notable are shops specialising in design articles or restaurants meeting the new gastronomic tastes, promoted by means of stars of all classes.

Passeig de Gràcia.

The most remarkable of the buildings are those situated to the west between the streets of Consell de Cent and Aragó. In the modernist era when they were constructed these buildings led to the area being ironically dubbed as *discord corner.* They are the **Casa Lleó Morera,** the work of Domènech i Montaner, whose façade has been retouched to remedy the damage done by a high-handed rationalist reformer; the **Amatller,** of northern inspiration, built by Puig i Cadalfach, and the **Batlló,** a typical and magnificent Gaudí creation. Only the second of these houses may be entered, since it is nowadays a gallery of Hispanic art: the **Instituto Amatller de Arte Hispánico.** It is only here, therefore, where the visitor may see the ornamental details with which these three great exponents of modernism decorated their buildings, according to the concept of total art they upheld. Nonetheless the mere contemplation of the façades will more than repay the visit, above all if the visitor manages to figure out which of the meanings that have been proposed for the Gaudí facade is closest to reality.

Visitors to **Casa Milà,** nicknamed *la Pedrera* (the quarry), are luckier in that they can get to know this crowning work of Gaudí's genius in greater detail. It is set on the corner of Carrer de Provença, and may be entered not only to see the *Espacio Gaudí,* which today comprises the upper part and its terrace, but also to see the art exhibitions put on in the building's second floor. Lastly, the visitor should note, as he strolls down the street, that the lampposts adorning the roadside verges are reconstructions of the original designs of the constructor Pere Falqués, using the same modernist design and identical materials – iron structure and quartered marble for the benches.

Terrace of Casa Milá (Gaudí).

On the following page: façade of the Casa Milá or "La Pedrera" (Quarry) by Gaudí.

Espacio Gaudí, in Casa Milá.

Pinnacle of Casa Lleó Morera.

Staircase of Casa Batlló. ▶

Below: the central well of Casa Batlló.

Torre Bellesguard (Gaudí).

A MOVEMENT THAT CULMINATES IN GAUDÍ

In Catalonia the modernist movement took on a stylistic expression somewhat different from elsewhere in Europe, for example in the *French Art Nouveau*. Catalan modernists set out to give their work a distinctive stamp of identity across the board, in architecture, decoration, painting, sculpture and literature.

Just as it enjoyed a boom between the late C19th and the early C20th, modernism then suffered a fierce critical backlash, taken to extreme lengths by the adherents of the International Modern Style, who opposed their own basically rationalist concepts to what they bluntly dismissed as mere frivolity. But today the surviving manifestations of that *total art* are justly appreciated and even exalted anew. Barcelona has come out of this well, as the recognised prime exponent of the movement in Spain, and therefore with a healthy stock of representative buildings dotted around the whole city.

A heavy concentration of them, mainly terrace houses, are to be found in the so-called *Quadrat d'or,* an ample area spreading throughout the whole Ensanche.

But the best way to get an overview of the movement in a brief visit is to limit yourself to the most important creations.

Casa Vicens (Gaudí).

*Below: Casa Terrades or "Les Punxes"
(Puig i Cadalfach).*

Colegio de las Teresianas (Gaudí).

The sculpture "Núvol i cadira" (Cloud and Seat) crowns the Fundación Tàpies. ▶

Avinguda Diagonal.

Preceding double page: Palau del Orfeó Catalá (Domènech i Montaner).

Examples of the profuse output of Domènech i Montaner include the following works: the facade of the **Editorial Montaner i Simon** on Carrer de Aragó, still topped with the wire crest that Tàpies chose as the stamp of the Foundation that occupies it - the interior is now a museum; the **Zoology Museum** set in the Parc de la Ciutadella; the **Casa Thomas,** headquarters of a design studio on Carrer Mallorca; the **Fonda Hotel España,** on Carrer de Sant Pau, whose restaurant gives you the chance of a close inspection of the exquisitely decorated interior; the **Palau del Orfeó Català** (Catalan Music Hall) on the corner of Carrer de Sant Pere Més Alt and Carrer Armadeu Vivies, an apotheosis of modernist exuberance, which you can easily enter merely by going to one of the concerts held there, for example the highly recommendable one given by the City Symphonic Orchestra every Saturday afternoon; the aforementioned **Casa Lleó Morera,** respectfully restored by the team of Óscar Tusquets, who is also the author of the contemporary details of the above-mentioned Palau del Orfeó Català; the **Hospital de Sant Pau,** on Avinguda de Sant Antoni María Claret, one of the towering works of the movement, whose pavilions may be visited on set days and times; and the **Palau Montaner,** still standing on Carrer de Mallorca and now housing the Central Government Department.

Examples of Puig i Cadafalch's work, with its northern inspiration, can be found in the Casa Martí on Carrer Montsió, better known for the café it houses, the *Quatre Gats,* famous artists' café of the period faithfully restored in honour of the artists who gathered there; the **Casa Amatller;** the **Palau Macaya** on Passeig de Sant Joan, cultural centre of La Caixa; the **Casa Terrades** on Avinguda Diagonal or **Les Punxes** as it is known, private in character and therefore revealing only the ornamental richness of its lobbies; the **Casa Serra** on the upper part of la Rambla de Catalunya, headquarters of the Barcelona Council, joining onto a building of contrasting contemporary lines; and the **Casa del Baró de Quadras,** also on Avinguda Diagonal, accessible by visiting the Music Museum it houses.

The sculpture "Terra i foc" (earth and fire) by Gardy-Artigas in front of the Caixa building on Avinguda Diagonal.

Below: Passeig de Lluís Companys, with the Triumphal Arch in the background.

*Hospital de Sant Pau
(Domènech i Montaner).*

Again, in the case of Gaudí, it is not possible to lay down a precise route to take in all his works in the city. These include the privately owned **Casa Vicens** on Carrer de Carolines, with captivating ceramic arabesques; the **Torre Bellesguard,** on the street of the same name, with an identical character; the **Casa Calvet,** on Carrer de Casp, in which an haute cuisine restaurant on the ground floor has had the good taste to preserve the Gaudian decoration of the original premises; the pavilions of **Finca Güell,** on Avinguda de Pedralbes, with the formidable wrought-iron dragon protecting the entrance gate; the **Palau Güell,** on Carrer Nou de la Rambla, occupied by the Theatre Institute, with its sensational leisure room, worth any effort to get to see it: the **Convento de las Teresianas,** on Carrer de Ganduxer, where, by previous appointment, you can visit one of Gaudí's most exquisite creations: a passageway of sinuously pointed arches; plus the aforementioned **Casa Batlló and Casa Milà** on Passeig de Gràcia.

*The highlight of the Palau del Orfeó Catalá
is the stained glass.*

*Modernist bakery
in Carrer de Girona.*

Two of Gaudi's most important works remain to be mentioned, exceptional both in size and quality: the **Parc Güell** and the unfinished **Templo de la Sagrada Familia** (Expiatory Temple of the Sacred Family), each one worth a whole day's visit in itself, or at least enough time to dwell on their exceptional details. They are to be found, respectively, on Carrer de Olot and Carrer de Mallorca. Today there is also an invaluable aid to understanding these crowning works of the modernist movement, both the architecture itself and the historical environment and character of its brilliant creator: the *Espacio Gaudí,* a set of audiovisuals, documents and models and serially arranged slides, accompanied by explanatory texts in several languages that the Caixa de Catalunya has set up in the upper part of *La Pedrera.*

It includes a visit to the famous terrace to see the outlandish forms of the smoke outlets and the layout of the inner courtyard. A real find and an absolute must.

Terrace of Palau Güell, by Gaudí.

Main gate of the Finca Güell.

*Above: detail of the mosaic ("tren cadis")
in Parc Güell.*

Parc Güell. Stairway leading to the hypostyle hall.

*Below: rustic colonnade of Parc Güell,
showing the influence
of rural Catalan constructions.*

◄ *Panoramic view of the Templo de la Sagrada Familia,
with the main front by Gaudí.*

*Right: Façade of the Nacimiento
(birth) by Gaudí.*

*Below: other details of the temple's exterior.
Right: the new sculptures by Subirachs.*

THE CITY'S SECOND GARDEN

The **Parc de la Ciutadella** has a military past that has gradually been dispelled down the ages as the fortifications were demolished, the ghost finally being laid to rest with the handing over of the park to the city in 1869. The holding of the 1888 Universal Exhibition here brought about its radical transformation, and in 1920 the French landscape gardener Forestier converted it into the second great green area of Barcelona. It is quite a walk to take it all in, but well worth the effort to wander down its wide avenues and appreciated its well-cared for plantlife, most examples of which are duly labelled. The park is studded with statues, monuments and fountains. The Passeig de Pujades entrance takes us straight to the **Zoological Museum** at the first crossway, built in brick by Domènech i Montaner to serve as a restaurant for that Exhibition and baptised at that time with the playful name of *Castell dels Tres Dragons* (Castle of the Three Dragons). The Greenhouse and the Shaded Hot House, the latter serving as a tropical botanical garden, are both modernist glass and metal structures. The adjacent **Geological Museum** is Neoclassical. The central part boasts a spectacular waterfall, the work of another of the park's creators, Josep Fontseré. The sculptural work was done between 1875 and 1861 by outstanding artists of the time, and the general design was the work of the young Gaudí just starting out on his career.

Parc de la Ciutadella. Waterfall.

Zoology Museum or "Castell dels Tres Dragons" (Castle of the Three Dragons) by Domènech i Montaner.

An artificial lake, a musical carousel and the curious bulk of a mammoth adorn the surroundings. The old Plaça de Armas, converted into a garden area, has a lake as centrepiece, featuring a copy of *Desconsol*, the famous sculpture by Llimona. At the back of the park the Palau del Parlament de Catalunya (Catalunya Parliament Building) can be visited only on a few special days, except for the part occupied by the Modern Art Museum. The thought-provoking exhibits of this museum give an overview of the modernist movement in painting, sculpture, precious metal work and furniture.

Lastly, in the eastern part of the park, the **Zoo,** rather cramped for space according to the tenets of today's ecologists, is nonetheless worth a look, if only to see its star billing, the albino gorilla *Copito de Nieve* (snowflake), a veritable symbol of the city. Another symbol, this time a delicate statue, is the *Dama del Paraguas* (lady with umbrella) that crowns a fountain in the same part.

The symbolic "Dama del Paraguas" in the Parc de la Ciutadella.

Parc del Laberinto de Horta.

Barcelona Zoo. "Snowflake", the albino gorilla.

Night-time on Passeig de Colom.

THE GATEWAY TO THE SEA

The radical transformation that the Barcelona coastline has undergone, including a large part of the port zone, has provided the city with an outstanding area for leisure, eating out and tourism. The main interest of the Portal de la Pau has always been the **Columbus Monument,** with the lift that takes you up to a lookout up top. It is also still possible to cross the port in a ferry or soar over it in a cable car. But now new attractions have been added to draw people in, very much to be taken into account on weekend visits.

Above: Port Vell and the Barceloneta district.

Below: night-time on the port with the Maremágnum centre.

To get to the to old Muelle de España (Spanish Wharf) today a sort of "golden peninsula", you can either take the car, which is then rather difficult to park, or cross by foot over the Rambla del Mar, a moving wooden bridge that is an attraction in itself. In the foreground stands the **Maremágnum** centre with a host of shops, bars and restaurants, both haute cuisine and those that seek an added charm in a cinema-inspired design.

The *Multicine* cinema has no less than eight projection rooms, whereas the Imax offers three types of screen: big screen, semispherical and three-dimensional.

Lastly, the **Centre de Mar** will undoubtedly prove the main attraction with its Aquarium, one of the best of its type in Europe, both in terms of the fish on show, mainly Mediterranean ones with the odd dogfish, and for the direct view it offers and the sheer size of the tanks. The Marina del Port Vell then links up with the Muelle de la Barceloneta, where the Palau de Mar stands. This houses the Museu d'Historia de Catalunya (Catalan History Museum), equipped with all the technological advances to enhance its monographic and national contents. But under the arches there is also a throng of restaurants, whose seafood cooking vies with those also concentrated nearby: on the wharves of **Port Olímpic,** to the west of the promenade.

Preceding double page: bird's eye view of Barcelona Port.

Below: the Port at night.

Port walkway.

This port zone, set apart from the shopping area that is an attraction in itself, ends up in the **Moll de la Fusta,** which runs parallel to the Passeig de Colom.

Various public shows are put on in the lower esplanade, while the cafés and restaurants of the upper fringe, amongst which one decorated with a huge shrimp by Mariscal stands out, share the selfsame attraction of the other ones of the area: the views they offer of the beguiling gateway to the sea.

La Rambla de Mar.

View of Port Vell of Barcelona.

Olympic port.

*The old port cable car,
traditional lookout over the city.*

Below: panorama of the Barceloneta district.

THE HILL OF JUPITER

The **Montaña de Montjuic** (Montjuic Hill), the Roman *Mons Jovis,* has always been an inseparable part of the landscape and history of Barcelona, and today it offers a variety of different attractions. The entrance via Plaça d' Espanya and Avinguda de la Reina María Cristina takes you in to the tradefair site, which stages important exhibitions throughout the year. At the entrance two towers that served as gateway to the International Exhibition of 1929 still fulfil a similar function today, ushering you in to the various pavilions that host the international fairs and exhibitions.

At the end of this avenue several escalators take you up to the foot of the **Palau Nacional,** a monumental building raised for the above event. Though striking in appearance, it is often reviled by certain critics, who accuse it of a botched eclecticism. It has nonetheless been fitted out as the **National Catalan Art Museum (MNAC),** to house one of the most important collections of Romanesque art in the world, together with other significant exhibits. The famous luminous fountains of Buïgas, which round off the general effect with their play of water and light, are only set working intermittently.

At the beginning of Avinguda del Marqués de Comillas stands the **Barcelona Pavilion** of *Mies Van der Rohe,* a must for all those who wish to see one of the pioneer works of rationalist architecture.

Monument to the sardana (traditional dance), on Montjuïc.

Avinguda de la Reina María Cristina with the Palau Nacional in the background. ▶

*Gothic panel in the National Catalan
Art Museum (MNAC).*

Night-time on the Avinguda de la Reina María Cristina.

Palau Sant Jordi (Arata Isozaki). In the background, Torre de Telecomunicaciones, by Santiago Calatrava.

Fundación Joan Miró. ▶

1992 Olympic stadium.

The same route, long enough to justify taking a car, leads us on to the Poble Espanyol (Spanish Village), still functioning as an compendium of characteristic streets and squares of different Spanish regions, although leisure sites and restaurants have been gradually eating into the ground occupied by handicrafts workshops, which used to give it more of a popular character. Avinguda del Estadi ends up at the Olympic Complex, with Bofill's Neoclassical INEFC building, the **Palau Sant Jordi,** an avant garde construction of Arata Isozaki and the refurbished Olympic Stadium.

A little to the east stands the **Fundación Joan Miró,** a thought-provoking building on many levels, firstly as a museum of contemporary painting and sculpture and obviously an anthology of Miro's work, and secondly for the clear Mediterranean definition of the building, with an exquisite design by Josep Maria Sert. To get to the castle, from within whose walls you can enjoy sweeping views together with a visit to a notable Military Museum, you can use the funicular, which strikes out from Avinguda Militar, or follow the road that climbs up to the right of it. The last word should go to the abundance of gardens that win the hill the distinction of the city's main green area. The most important of them are the gardens of **Joan Maragall,** with their statues surrounding the Palacete Albéniz, the Botanical Gardens, on the western slope and, on the opposite side, the gardens of Mossèn Costa i Llobera, of great value for their collection of cacti and exotic species.

Gardens of Joan Maragall.

◀ *Night-time view of the Palau Nacional on Montjuic.*

Parc de la Espanya Industrial, a haven of peace in the Barcelona metropolis.

◄ *Parc del Escorxador, with the sculpture "Dona i Ocell" by Joan Miró.*

AN OPEN-AIR MUSEUM

As part of the challenge of hosting the 1992 Olympics, and even before this honour, Barcelona commissioned artists and architects of the most diverse styles to fill new and old spots of the city with examples of their work.

These artists, some of them belonging to the most avant garde trends, were thus encouraged to express their creativity in the planning and lay out of city spaces, in the construction of buildings and urban features and, above all, in the creation of striking sculptures.

One of the most important of the squares, as a example of the so called rigid type, is the **Plaça de los Països Catalans,** opposite the Barcelona-Sants Train Station, distinguished by the University of Harvard. The parks can be represented by the Parc de la **Espanya Industrial,** close to the former, with its leisure lake; the Parc Joan Miró, or **Escorxador,** whose esplanade on the Carrer de Tarragona side boasts a colourful Miró statue called *Dona i Ocell* (Women and bird); the **Estación del Norte** close to Carrer de la Marina, where we can admire the *Cel Caigut* and the *Espiral arbrada* of Beverly Pepper; and the Parc de la **Creueta del Coll,** in the district of Carmel, where the *Elogio del Agua* by Eduardo Chillida hangs.

Street view in the Olympic Village.

Below: beach of the Olympic Village.

The best sculptures can be found in the Vall de Hebron (*Mistos* – Matches – by Oldenburg and Van Broggen, and *Dime, dime querido* – Do tell me my love – by Susana Solano); in the gardens surrounding the Velódromo de Horta (*Poema Visual*, by Joan Brossa); at the entrance to the Olympic Village (*Pez,* - fish - by Frank O'Ghery, opposite the skyscraper of the Hotel Les Arts), and in the Plaça de Antonio López (*Cabeza de Barcelona* – Head of Barcelona, by Roy Lichtenstein). The most important of the buildings and town planning schemes are the **Torre de Collserola,** by Norman Foster; the Torre de **Telecomunicaciones,** in the Olympic Complex, and the **Puente de Bac de Roda,** both by Santiago Calatrava; the **Palau Sant Jordí,** in the same complex, by Irata Isozaki and lastly the group of buildings making up the **Olympic Village,** a newly created district with a multiple, global design. The **Barcelona Contemporary Art Museum (MACBA),** an original and controversial building by Richard Meier, in the district of El Raval, serves as a compendium of these innovatory trends that have made Barcelona a veritable open-air museum.

The buildings of the newly developed area called Nova Icària, next to what was the Olympic Village, bring us to the very brink of the C21st.

Barcelona Contemporary Art Museum (MACBA).

THE "MAGIC MOUNTAIN"

Any visit to Barcelona just has to be finished off with the panoramic view of the city to be gained from the vantage point on the top of Mount **Tibidado.** It is set beside a fairground, whose rides and thrills are evermore sophisticated affairs. There are two ways of reaching it by car, either by following the Sarriá-Vallvidrera road or the road from Arrabassada in the opposite direction. Another slower but perhaps more attractive means of approach is to take the *Tramvia Blau* (Blue Tram), which leaves from the beginning of Avinguda del Tibidabo, then continuing by funicular.

At the peak, the temple of Sagrado Corazón, a fairly poor Neogothic imitation, and the dated but original Automaton Museum, are the site's main features. Close by, the spiky tower of Collserola prints its spectacular silhouette on the backdrop of the city. Lower down, the Fabra Observatory occupies a privileged spot on the hillside.

View of Barcelona from Mount Tibidabo.

Torre de Collserola by Norman Foster.

Three evocative pictures of the city of Barcelona to end with:

Above: book stalls on *Día de Sant Jordi (Saint George's Day).*

◀ *A human tower being built by "Castellers" on Plaça de Sant Jaume.*

Below: Sardanas being danced outside the Cathedral.